STREAMLINERS TO THE TWIN CITIES

PHOTO ARCHIVE

400, Twin Zephyrs, & Hiawatha Trains

John Kelly

Iconografix
Photo Archive Series

Iconografix
PO Box 446
Hudson, Wisconsin 54016 USA

Library of Congress Card Number: 2002115431

ISBN 1-58388-096-8

03 04 05 06 07 08 09 5 4 3 2 1

Printed in China

Cover and book design by Shawn Glidden

Copyediting by Suzie Helberg

COVER PHOTO: Chicago & North Western train No.203 (Minneapolis-Omaha), crossing the James J. Hill Stone Arch Bridge after departing Minneapolis Great Northern Station. *JM Gruber collection*

BOOK PROPOSALS

Iconografix is a publishing company specializing in books for transportation enthusiasts. We publish in a number of different areas, including Automobiles, Auto Racing, Buses, Construction Equipment, Emergency Equipment, Farming Equipment, Railroads & Trucks. The Iconografix imprint is constantly growing and expanding into new subject areas.

Authors, editors, and knowledgeable enthusiasts in the field of transportation history are invited to contact the Editorial Department at Iconografix, Inc., PO Box 446, Hudson, WI 54016.

TABLE OF CONTENTS

ACKNOWLEDGMENTS

This book is dedicated to my Father and Mother, Jack and Eleanor Kelly, for taking me on Sunday car rides along the Upper Mississippi River to view Zephyrs and Hiawathas in the 1950s.

Thank you to the following friends for the use of their timeless photos and collections: JM Gruber, Paul Knutson, Bruce Meyer, Mike and Mark Nelson, Bill Raia, Jay Williams, Rich Worisek, Douglas Wornom; to Suzanne Burris, Curator/Archivist, BNSF Railway, Fort Worth, Texas, for assistance on the Burlington Route; to Joan Metzger, Assistant University Archivist, Northern Illinois University, for help on the Chicago & North Western. Special thanks to John Gruber (Railroad Heritage) and Matt Van Hattem (Trains.com) for giving me the opportunities to write on the Streamlined Era; to Dylan Frautschi, Managing Editor and the staff at Iconografix, Incorporated, for guiding me through the book process; finally, to my "in-house" editor, partner and best friend, Linda Marie Shult, for her love, support and encouragement of this book.

Several photographs selected for this book include railroad employees. In my opinion, it is the train crews, dining car staff, porters and conductors all working together that makes your train trip enjoyable. So "All Aboard" for the Twin Cities of St. Paul-Minneapolis.

I hope you enjoy your ride on the 400, Zephyrs and Hiawatha.

John Kelly
Madison, Wisconsin
October 2002

INTRODUCTION

In 1935, an intense rivalry between the Chicago & North Western, Milwaukee Road and Burlington Route began in the busy Chicago-St. Paul/Minneapolis (Twin Cities) corridor. The competition lasted until 1971. For many years the proud 400s, bold Hiawathas and sleek Zephyrs held the fastest start-to-stop running times in the world. Each railroad had its own route, but all three had the same goal: to carry the maximum number of passengers between Chicago and the Twin Cities in the shortest amount of time. Which one of these trains was the swiftest? The speed of all three trains was timed frequently, and each of them broke the 100-mph limit almost daily. So each train was the fastest at one time or another.

All of this really began in 1934, when Chicago, Burlington & Quincy premiered its new streamlined Zephyr 9900 on the now famous dawn-to-dusk, 1,015-mile, Denver-Chicago run. Shortly after the Zephyr 9900's debut, Burlington announced it would operate Zephyr type trains between Chicago and the Twin Cities. The Milwaukee Road declared it would meet Burlington's challenge with a new streamlined, steam-powered train. Chicago & North Western also planned to improve its Chicago-Twin Cities service, but gave no details. All three roads said they would cut their Chicago-Twin Cities operating schedules from 10.5 hours to 7.5 hours.

On January 2, 1935, Chicago & North Western (C&NW) was the first of the three roads to offer high-speed, Chicago-Twin Cities service. Departing westbound from C&NW Chicago Passenger Terminal, led by 4-6-2 Pacific, oil-fired steam locomotives with upgraded heavyweight, air-conditioned cars, the train was scheduled to run "400 miles in 400 minutes," hence the name 400 (the actual timetable distance from Chicago to St. Paul was 408.6 miles). Initially, the 400 had no maximum speed limits, and 100-plus mph was the usual speed on the Evanston-Milwaukee segment. This allowed the 400 to use the slogan "The Train That Set The Pace For The World." Upon arrival in Milwaukee, the 400 stopped at the C&NW Romanesque style depot situated on the city's waterfront at the edge of Lake Michigan. Leaving Milwaukee, the 400 raced past the bucolic farmlands and villages of central Wisconsin on its journey to the Twin Cities. On September 24, 1939, C&NW introduced a brand-new, streamlined 400 in apple green and English stagecoach yellow livery. C&NW advertising described it as the finest train built by Pullman-Standard.

The Burlington Twin Zephyrs debuted next, on April 21, 1935. Nos. 9901 and 9902 were three-car articulated, Budd-built, stainless steel trains. The rakish, shovelnose locomotives contained a 600-horsepower, eight-cylinder Winton engine and 28-foot baggage compartment. The second car had a kitchen, lunch-counter and 40 coach seats. The third car had 24 coach seats and 24 parlor chairs for total seating of 88. The shiny trains began service with one trip in each direction between Chicago and the Twin Cities. However, the reserved-seat trains were in such demand that after only two months of revenue service, the Twin Zephyrs (later renamed Morning Zephyr and Afternoon Zephyr) switched to daily round trips. Leaving from Chicago Union Station westbound, the Zephyrs raced 38 miles to Aurora, Illinois, where the main line diverged to Galesburg or Savanna, Illinois. From Savanna, the Zephyrs turned north for a swift ride along the east bank of the Mississippi River with stops at East Dubuque, Illinois, Prairie du Chien, La Crosse and Winona Junction, Wisconsin. Burlington brochures touted its route along the Upper Mississippi River as the "Mississippi River Scenic Line – Where Nature Smiles 300 Miles." The trains then sprinted up-river to Prescott, Wisconsin, where the rails bridged the St. Croix River on single track. At St. Croix Tower near Hastings, Minnesota, the CB&Q and Milwaukee Road main lines converged and both railroads pooled their parallel, single trackage to form joint, double-track for 19 miles into St. Paul Union Depot.

The Zephyr name was coined by Ralph Budd, (President of Burlington Lines), after reading Chaucer's Canterbury Tales, where Zephyrus was the mythical "God of West Wind." On December 18, 1936, two new, eight-car articulated Twin Zephyrs entered service. Pegasus 9904 and Zephyrus 9905 led the highly publicized "Train of the Gods and Goddesses." For years the Morning Zephyr-No.21, had the fastest overall start-to-stop running time in the world, 84 mph between East Dubuque, Illinois, and Prairie du Chien, Wisconsin. This timing enabled the Morning Zephyr to make the 427-mile Chicago-St. Paul run in an even six hours. The Twin Zephyrs symbolized speed, service and a new era for the Burlington Route.

On May 29, 1935, the Milwaukee Road inaugurated the Hiawatha, named after the Native American in Longfellow's "Song of Hiawatha" poem. Chicago Union Station was the departure point for westbound No.101. Eastbound No.100 departed from Minneapolis. Led by Alco-built, Class-A Atlantic 4-4-2 streamlined, oil-fired steam locomotives, each Hiawatha offered luxury rail travel in the 410-mile Chicago-St. Paul corridor. Later renamed Morning Hiawatha and Afternoon Hiawatha, the trains were styled in blazing Art Deco orange, maroon and gray colors. Steel cars were handcrafted in Milwaukee Shops and had fantastic names, such as Tip Top Tap (named after Tip Top Inn at the top of the Pullman building in Chicago), and Beaver Tail parlor-observation, the train's signature car. Fast running always occurred between Wisconsin Dells and Lyndon Station, referred to as "Speedway of the Speedliners," where the superb Milwaukee Atlantics often reached speeds of 100 mph. After crossing the Mississippi River at La Crosse, Wisconsin, the Hiawathas followed the main line along the west bank of the river. Magnificent river scenery was viewed along the expanse of river between Winona and Red Wing, Minnesota. Sweeping curved trackage passes beneath steep limestone bluffs offered terrific river views. From Red Wing, the Hiawathas continued up-river to St. Croix Tower, where the Milwaukee rails converged with the CB&Q main line and headed into St. Paul, Minnesota. The Milwaukee Road continued its streamlined look in 1948, when it premiered Skytop observation cars on the Hiawatha trains. And in 1952 they introduced the Super Dome, full-length, glass-roofed dome cars built by Pullman-Standard.

Upon arrival in the Twin Cities, the 400s, Zephyrs and Hiawathas all stopped at St. Paul Union Depot. Originally built in 1883, destroyed by fire in 1913 and rebuilt in 1920, St. Paul Union Depot is located along the Mississippi River levee at the edge of downtown St. Paul. Union Depot was and still is a grand structure with ten commanding stone columns guarding the front entrance. Inside the three-story structure, ornate marble floors covered the football field-sized concourse. The depot housed the offices of Northern Pacific's dining car department, a post office, USO Club, bowling alley, restaurant and gift shop. Beyond the concourse, escalators carried passengers down to track level, where 22 arrival-departure tracks had butterfly-type canopies. The "Golden Years" for St. Paul Union Depot was the period from 1920 to the late 1950s. In the early 1920s, Union Depot hosted over 250 arrivals and departures daily. The depot served as a major Twin Cities hub for nine Midwest railroads including Burlington, Milwaukee Road, Great Northern, Northern Pacific, Rock Island, Chicago & North Western, Chicago Great Western, Soo Line, and Minneapolis & St. Louis. Postwar streamlining added to the colorful mix of passenger trains passing through Union Depot. After departing St. Paul, it took the railroads approximately 30 minutes to reach Minneapolis. The 400s and Zephyrs both terminated at Great Northern Station on Hennepin Avenue, situated on the east bank of the Mississippi River in Minneapolis. The Hiawathas used their own station on Washington and Third Avenues in downtown Minneapolis. Eventually, travelers between Chicago and the Twin Cities could choose from a whole fleet of trains including 400, Zephyrs, Hiawatha, Empire Builder, North Coast Limited, Western Star, Mainstreeter, plus overnight trains Pioneer Limited and Blackhawk.

Without question the 400s, Zephyrs and Hiawathas wrote a colorful and significant chapter into American railroad history. These trains were the forerunners of today's high-speed rail movement. Despite their speed records, styling, comfort and initial earnings, the trains lost the competition to the automobile, interstate highways and airlines. Ridership steadily declined into the 1960s. On April 30, 1971, the last train to depart from St. Paul Union Depot was No.9, westbound Afternoon Zephyr. This marked the end of private passenger train service to the Twin Cities and the beginning of Amtrak.

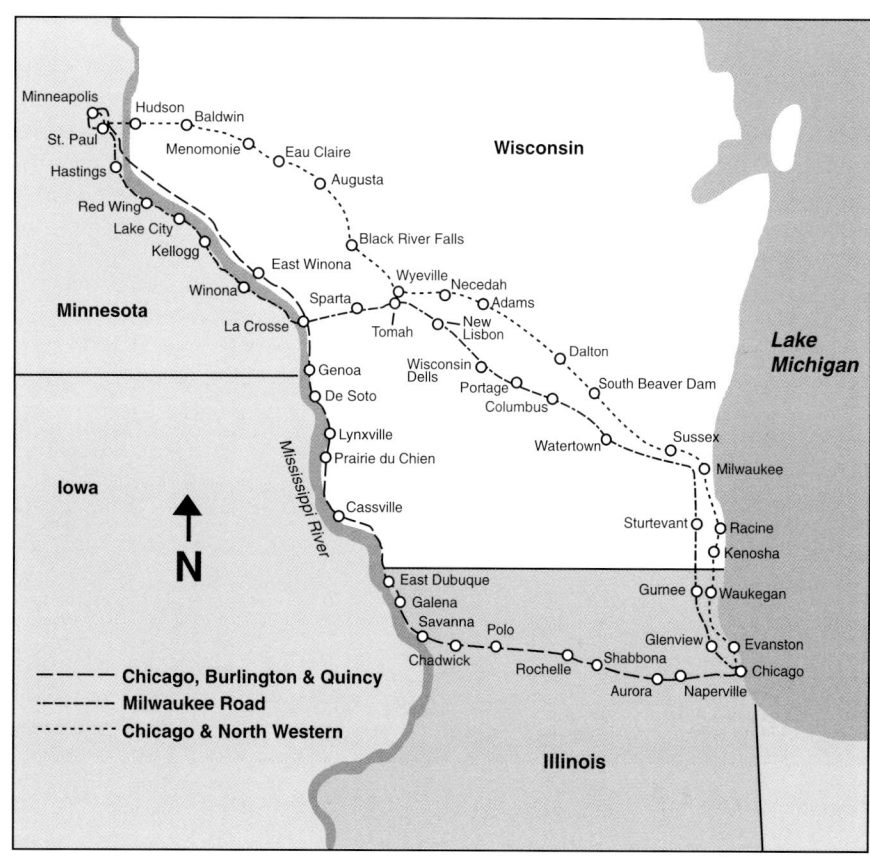

Chicago Union Station information desk, June 28, 1934. Note the train board information and the Fred Harvey cafeteria sign above the clock. *JM Gruber collection*

Chicago Union Station opened May 15, 1925, and hosted trains of four major railroads in Chicago: Chicago, Burlington & Quincy, Milwaukee Road, Pennsylvania Railroad, and Gulf, Mobile & Ohio Railroad. View is looking toward the south side of the depot. *JM Gruber collection*

Chicago & North Western Passenger Terminal at Madison and Canal Streets in downtown Chicago opened January 3, 1911. The terminal had 16-platform tracks, accessed by six approach tracks under an 894-foot train shed. *Northern Illinois University Archives*

Chicago & North Western 1940 passenger timetable for the Streamlined 400. *Author's collection*

A bird's-eye view of C&NW Chicago Avenue freight and coach yard. This was one of several C&NW Chicago area yards. *JM Gruber collection*

Burlington Route 1935 passenger timetable for the Twin Zephyrs. *Author's collection*

The Twin Cities Zephyrs were christened April 15, 1935, at Chicago Union Station by 13-year-old twin sisters, Frances and Marion Beeler. *BNSF Archives*

On April 16, 1935, the original Twin Cities Zephyrs 9901 and 9902 posed for the company photographer at Chicago Union Station. *BNSF Archives*

The Burlington Route herald was proudly displayed at the road's service facility, known locally as the "Zephyr Pit" on Canal Street, south of Roosevelt Road in Chicago. *July 1936, Grant Oaks photo, JM Gruber collection*

Milwaukee Road 1935 Hiawatha travel brochure. By November 1935, the Hiawatha had carried 100,000 passengers and became the passengers' streamliner of choice in terms of patronage. *Author's collection*

The MILWAUKEE ROAD *presents* THE FIRST OF THE SPEEDLINERS · *Hiawatha*

CHICAGO MILWAUKEE ST. PAUL AND PACIFIC

CHICAGO MILWAUKEE ST. PAUL MINNEAPOLIS

AMERICA'S FIRST INTEGRAL STREAMLINED STEAM LOCOMOTIVE AND THE NEWEST TYPE OF STREAM-STYLED SUPER-SPEED TRAIN

The curious crowd gathered at Chicago Union Station to view Milwaukee Road's newly designed Hudson 4-6-4 locomotive, October 17, 1938. *JM Gruber collection*

Milwaukee Road Atlantic 4-4-2
No. 4, ready to depart Chicago Union
Station with the Olympian. *JM
Gruber collection*

Spit and polish was the order of the day at Milwaukee Road's Western Avenue engine facility in Chicago, April 1937. Atlantic 4-4-2 No.2, built by American Locomotive Company, powered the Hiawathas. *JM Gruber collection*

Milwaukee Road's Atlantic 4-4-2 being fueled at Chicago's Western Avenue engine facility, April 1937. *JM Gruber collection*

Milwaukee Road Alco streamlined F7 Hudson 4-6-4 Hiawatha locomotive shown at Chicago, September 19, 1940. *JM Gruber collection*

Interior view of F7 Hudson cab showing speedometer, throttles, levers, gauges, brakes, and firebox. *Rich Worisek collection*

Milwaukee Road "Famous No. 15" EMD E6 at Western Avenue yard in Chicago. The diesels consisted of two cab units operated back-to-back. For many years engine No. 15 led the eastbound Hiawatha from Minneapolis. Then it would double back to the Twin Cities on overnight train No. 57, the Fast Mail. *JM Gruber collection*

Milwaukee Road Western Avenue yard and diesel facility in Chicago, June 27, 1970. *Owen Leander photo, Rich Worisek collection*

Milwaukee Road Skytop car "Dell Rapids" at Chicago, July 25, 1963. *Owen Leander photo, Rich Worisek collection*

Chicago Union Station was also home to the Milwaukee suburban commuter fleet. The West Line extended from Chicago to Elgin, Illinois, and the North Line from Chicago to Walworth, Illinois. Photo was taken on July 3, 1966. *Owen Leander photo, Rich Worisek collection*

Milwaukee Road Railway Post Office car, Carl F. Rank departing Chicago Union Station at Canal Street, June 4, 1967. *Owen Leander photo, Rich Worisek collection*

Milwaukee Road Railway Express Agency car in orange and maroon colors at Chicago, October 23, 1960. *Owen Leander photo, Rich Worisek collection*

Burlington Northern 9983 leads the combined westbound Empire Builder-North Coast Limited from Chicago Union Station, April 1971. The Pennsylvania Railroad Polk Street warehouse is in the background. View is from Roosevelt Road. *Doug Wornom photo*

Northern Pacific coach, painted in Raymond Loewy designed two-tone green colors, departing Chicago Union Station on the combined westbound Empire Builder-North Coast Limited, April 1971. *Doug Wornom photo*

Burlington Northern 9947 fronts the westbound Afternoon Zephyr from Chicago Union Station, April 1971. Note the three dome cars behind the baggage car. View is from Roosevelt Road. *Doug Wornom photo*

OCTOBER 26, 1958

CHICAGO
AND
NORTH WESTERN
RAILWAY

OCTOBER 26, 1958

CHICAGO
AND
NORTH WESTERN
RAILWAY

Famous For
PIGGY BACK
Freight Service

The Midwest's Finest Freight Service

Route of the FAMOUS
"400" **Streamliners**

Chicago & North Western 1958 public timetable with schedules of all 400 trains. *Author's collection*

Power for the original 400s were four Class E-2-a Pacific 4-6-2, oil-fired steam locomotives. Nos. 2902, 2903, 2907 and 2908 were built by American-Schenectady, and protected the schedules of trains 400 and 401 until dieselization in 1939. Locomotive 2908 is leading a fast 400 past Canal Tower at Evanston, Illinois. *Northern Illinois University Archives*

Heavyweight 78-foot C&NW cars "Odin" and "Viking" were drawing room-parlor-solarium cars built by the Pullman Company and used on the original 400 trains. The cars had green upholstery, small ornate metal luggage racks, and console radios probably playing the swing music of Benny Goodman or Tommy Dorsey. *Northern Illinois University Archives*

C&NW cars "Odin" and "Viking" contained 12-parlor seats forward, 5-passenger drawing room, 11-rear parlor seats and 8-seat solarium. Both cars carried the 400 drumheads suspended from the rear railing. *Northern Illinois University Archives*

C&NW streamlined the 400 on September 24, 1939. Photo shows E3 5002, leading westbound Twin Cities train No.401. *JM Gruber collection*

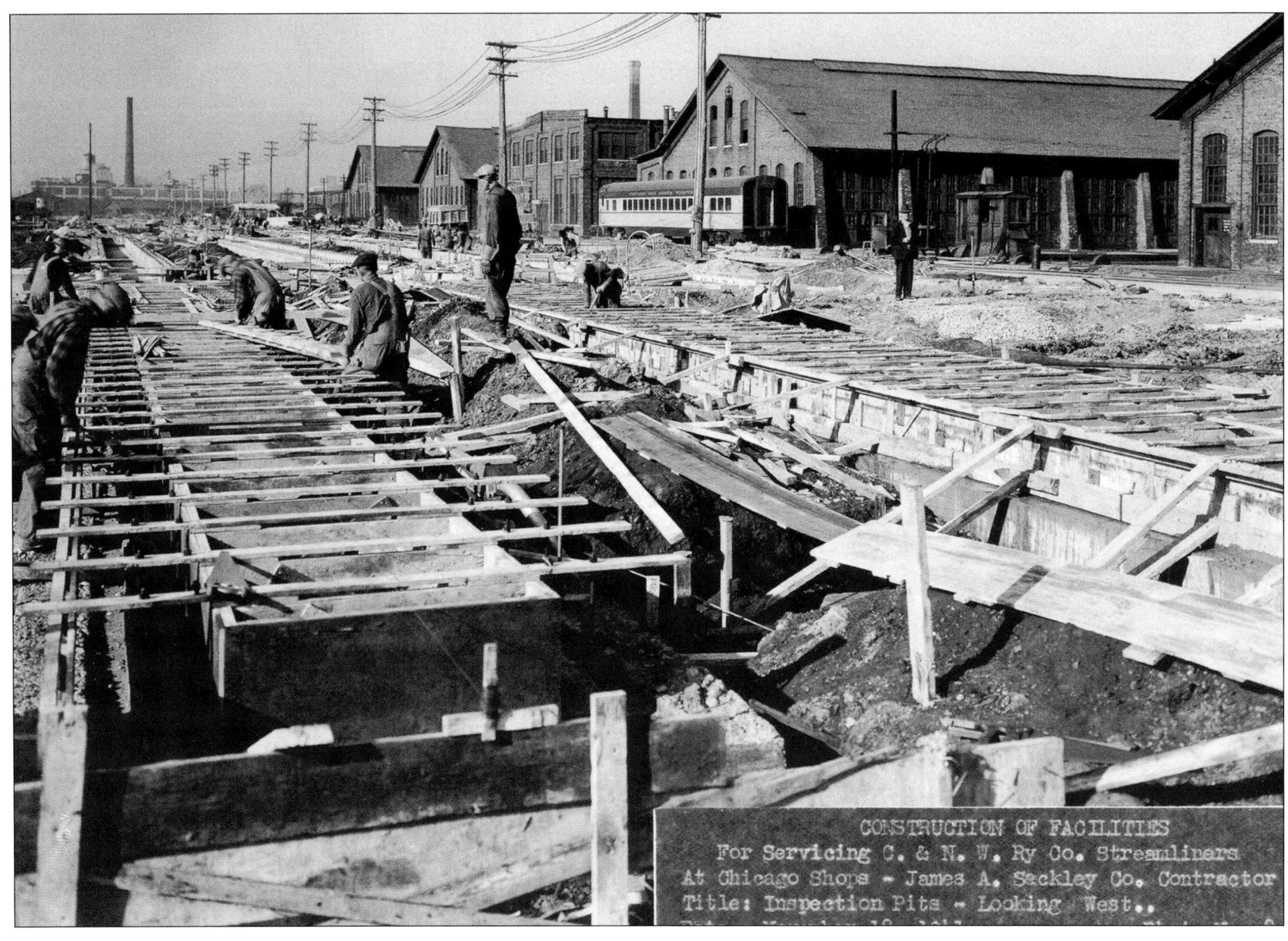

CONSTRUCTION OF FACILITIES
For Servicing C. & N. W. Ry Co. Streamliners
At Chicago Shops - James A. Seckley Co. Contractor
Title: Inspection Pits - Looking West..

Construction of C&NW streamliner service facility at 40th Street coach yard in Chicago, November 10, 1941. Just 19 days after this picture was taken, Pearl Harbor was bombed, December 7, 1941, and the United States entered World War II. *Northern Illinois University Archives*

C&NW streamliner facility at 40th Street coach yard in Chicago shows 400 being serviced in 1947. Union Pacific "Cities" trains were also maintained at 40th Street yard. *Northern Illinois University Archives*

C&NW chef Alec Broughton posed for the company photographer aboard the 400 dining car. Note the tasty dinner in pans about to be served to dining car passengers. *Northern Illinois University Archives*

Chicago & North Western System 1950s
dining car menu. *Author's collection*

C&NW train No.401 westbound at Kenosha, Wisconsin in 1946. C&NW timetables stated "Nos.400 and 401 are superior to all trains. Freight trains, transfer trains and switch engines must clear the schedules of Nos.400 and 401 [by] fifteen (15) minutes." *Northern Illinois University Archives*

C&NW train No.401 westbound arrived at Milwaukee and changed crews. Nos.400 and 401 also changed crews at Adams, Wisconsin. *Northern Illinois University Archives*

C&NW train No.401 westbound departed Milwaukee's lakefront depot for the Twin Cities. Lake Michigan is in the background of the photo. *Northern Illinois University Archives*

C&NW celebrated the 10th Anniversary of the 400 with special menus and decorative tablecloths depicting the road's famed "Pioneer" 4-2-0 locomotive. *Northern Illinois University Archives*

January 2, 1945, marked the 400's 10th Anniversary as Stewardesses pinned yellow roses, symbolizing the train's color, to women passengers that day at Chicago Passenger Terminal. 400 Stewardesses all wore dark blue gabardine, semi-military uniforms then in style for airline stewardesses, including white shirt, red tie and overseas cap with 400 insignia. *Northern Illinois University Archives*

400 Stewardess Dorothy Whitt talked to passengers aboard a streamlined 400 coach in 1939. Stewardess's duties included assistance to passengers and mothers traveling alone with children. *Northern Illinois University Archives*

C&NW lead car on the 400 was Art Deco style, baggage-tap-lounge car. The car's décor included large circular mirrors and ten stools upholstered in red leather with aluminum edging. In the lounge area, photomurals above the windows illustrated major cities served by the 400. *Northern Illinois University Archives*

Twin Cities No.401 and Dakota 400 meet at Wyeville, Wisconsin, September 1, 1958. The Dakota 400 route traversed western Wisconsin and eastern Minnesota. The train provided service from Chicago to Madison, Wisconsin, Rochester, Minnesota and Rapid City, South Dakota with intermediate stops. *Northern Illinois University Archives*

In October 1960 the Dakota 400 was renamed Rochester 400 with service from Chicago to Mankato, Minnesota. On June 23, 1963, just one month before the train was discontinued, eastbound No.518 Rochester 400 passes Wyeville Tower en route to Chicago. *John Gruber photo*

Eastbound No.518 Rochester 400 passengers detrain at Wyeville for connections with the westbound Twin Cities No.401 on June 23, 1963. *John Gruber photo*

400 Club Tavern – Altoona, Wisconsin, located across the street from the Chicago & North Western main line, "Route of the 400s." *Mark Nelson photo*

MISSISSIPPI RIVER

Scenic Line

HISTORIC HIGHWAY
OF THE MIDDLE WEST

MISSISSIPPI RIVER

Scenic Line

WHERE NATURE SMILES
THREE HUNDRED MILES

Burlington
Route

Burlington
Route

Burlington Route 1944 travel
brochure for the Mississippi
River Scenic Line. *Author's collection*

Train No.26 eastbound North Coast Limited with Burlington motive power passes Rochelle, Illinois, Tower in September 1963. *Mark Nelson photo*

Eastbound Twin Cities Zephyr, led by Pegasus 9904, boards passengers at Savanna, Illinois, September 15, 1938. No.9904 was built in November 1936. *JM Gruber collection*

Train No.22 eastbound Morning Zephyr was making good time south of Galena Junction, Illinois, on its journey to Chicago, August 5, 1967. *Mark Nelson photo*

Train No. 21 westbound Morning Zephyr passes Portage, Illinois. Between Portage and East Dubuque, Illinois, CB&Q had trackage rights over the Illinois Central Railroad for 13 miles. Photo taken on March 10, 1968. *Mark Nelson photo*

Burlington Route 1938 Twin Zephyrs travel brochures. *Author's collection*

Eastbound Twin Cities Zephyr, led by Pegasus 9904, boards passengers at East Dubuque, Illinois, September 15, 1938. No.9904 was scrapped at West Burlington, Iowa, August 1957. *JM Gruber collection*

After crossing the Mississippi River and Burlington Route trackage, Chicago Great Western 114-C, Oelwein-Chicago freight train exits the short tunnel at East Dubuque, Illinois, with 6 engines and 124 cars on April 11, 1968. *Mark Nelson photo*

Burlington E8 pulling No.21, the westbound Morning Zephyr, with six cars at East Dubuque, Illinois, April 1966. *Mark Nelson photo*

Combined westbound Afternoon Zephyr-Empire Builder crossing Sinsinawa River Bridge, near East Dubuque, Illinois, August 2, 1968. *Mark Nelson photo*

Second No.7 westbound Zephyr and combined 18-car train with Vista-Domes, skirts the east bank of the Mississippi River near East Dubuque, Illinois, August 2, 1969. *Mark Nelson photo*

Interior of second Twin Cities Zephyr dining car shows the elegant table settings with linen tablecloths and napkins, silverware and indirect lighting in the ceiling. The car seated 32 people for dinner with 4 at each table. *BNSF Archives*

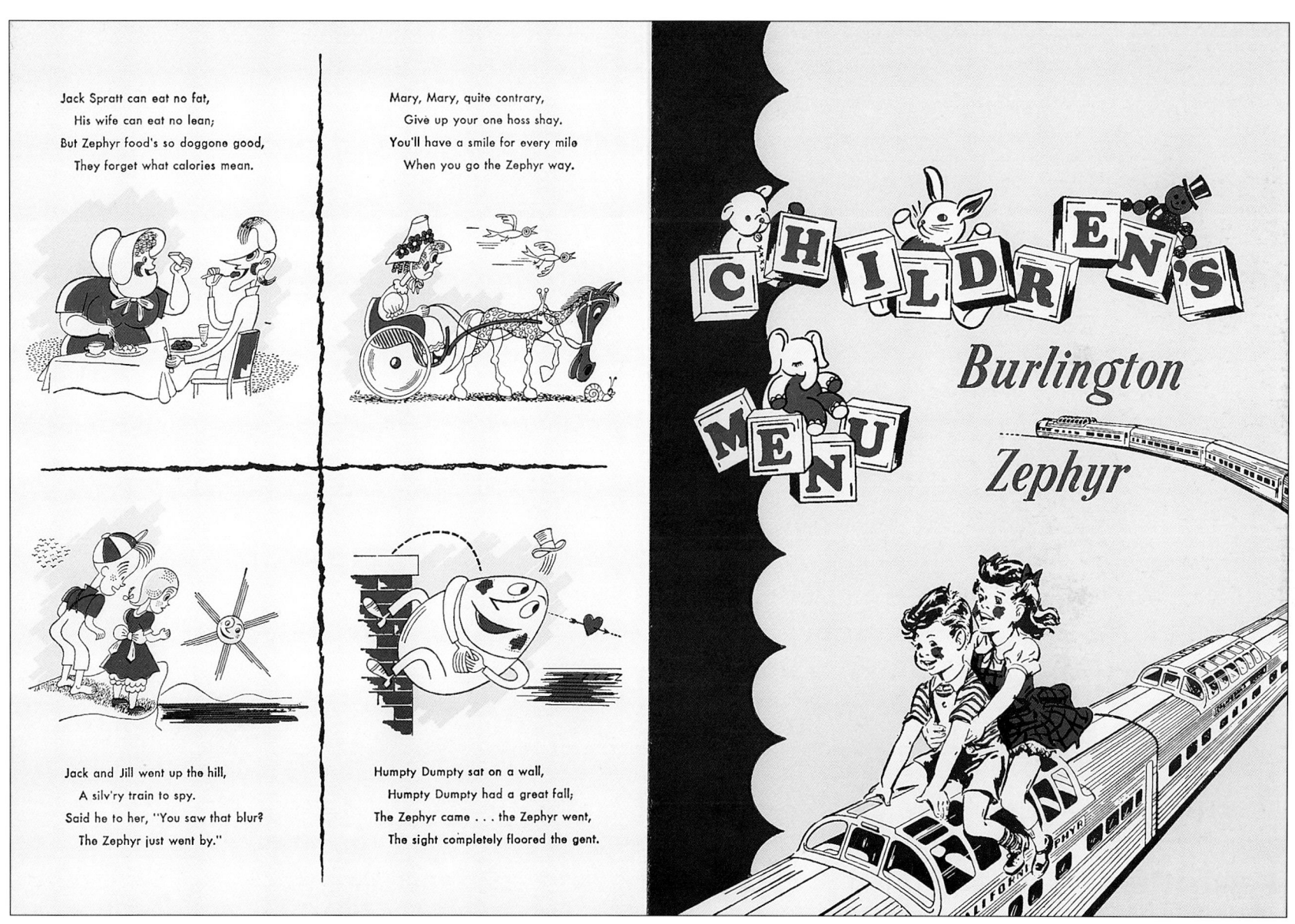

Burlington Route children's menu with nursery rhymes. *Author's collection*

"Silver Dome," the first modern dome car was built in Burlington's Aurora Shops from coach "Silver Alchemy." "Silver Dome's" first trip was on July 23, 1945, from Chicago to the Twin Cities on CB&Q train No. 45. *Owen Leander photo, JM Gruber collection*

December 19, 1947, Twin Cities Zephyr with E-unit and Vista-Dome combined with older articulated Zephyr cars. *BNSF Archives*

Twin Cities Zephyr in a scene from Burlington Route travel brochures along the Upper Mississippi River, "Where nature smiles for 300 miles." *BNSF Archives*

CHICAGO MILWAUKEE ST. PAUL AND PACIFIC

A New Masterpiece

THE NEW
Hiawatha

The MILWAUKEE ROAD   The MILWAUKEE ROAD

Milwaukee Road 1937 Hiawatha travel brochure. *Author's collection*

Milwaukee Road E7 16 posed for the company photographer with Hiawatha equipment. *Rich Worisek collection*

Milwaukee Road 30C rolls past Rondout, Illinois with substantial head end traffic. Terminal road Elgin, Joliet & Eastern's single track from Joliet to Waukegan, Illinois, crossed the Milwaukee Road trackage at Rondout Tower, June 8, 1967. *Owen Leander photo, Rich Worisek collection*

Milwaukee Road's hometown terminal was built in 1886 and fronted Everett Street, hence it was named Everett Street Depot. Always a busy urban depot, five tracks curved into and out of the train shed. The depot was razed in 1966. *Author's collection*

The train shed at Milwaukee's Everett Street Depot had 38C and bi-level coaches ready to depart, June 26, 1965. Note the bags of U.S. Mail on baggage carts waiting to be loaded on mail cars. *Owen Leander photo, Rich Worisek collection*

Powering the 1947 Chicago-Seattle Olympian Hiawatha were the Fairbanks-Morse passenger diesels, enhanced with chrome trim and lettering by Wisconsin industrial designer Brooks Stevens, March 26, 1947. *Milwaukee Road photo. JM Gruber collection*

Wisconsin industrial designer Brooks Stevens planned the beautiful Hiawatha Skytop observation cars in 1947, both in parlor-lounge and sleeper-lounge style. Pullman-Standard built ten of these cars for use on the Chicago-Twin Cities Hiawatha and the Chicago-Seattle Olympian Hiawatha. *Author's collection*

Milwaukee Road 1948 travel brochure for new Twin Cities Hiawathas. *Author's collection*

West end of Milwaukee Road Depot in Milwaukee shows the Afternoon Hiawatha led by Alco DL-109 14. *Author's collection*

Milwaukee Road 17B ready to leave Milwaukee, Wisconsin depot with westbound Morning Hiawatha, June 13, 1948. Note the Railway Express Agency office behind the locomotive. *Bill Raia collection*

Milwaukee Road 16A ready to depart Milwaukee, Wisconsin depot with eastbound Olympian Hiawatha, June 13, 1948. *Bill Raia collection*

Engine 94C was in the first group of FP7's delivered in 1950 and first FP7's to sport the stylized Hiawatha Indian with outstretched bow in hand, suggestive of swiftness. The logo was also used by the railroad on public timetable covers. Photo taken in Milwaukee, Wisconsin, August 1950. *JM Gruber collection*

Milwaukee Road Silver Anniversary dining car
menu. *Author's collection*

Milwaukee Road and Hiawatha Skytop car "Dell Rapids," approaching Milwaukee, Wisconsin, June 26, 1965. *Owen Leander photo, Rich Worisek collection*

Milwaukee Road Olympian Hiawatha travel brochure featuring the new Super Domes. *Author's collection*

"Delightfully new for a wonderful view" is how Milwaukee Road brochures described the new Pullman-Standard built Super Dome cars. The Super Domes entered service December 22, 1952. Six were assigned to the Olympian Hiawatha and four to the Chicago-Twin Cities Hiawatha. Photo was taken June 27, 1971. *Owen Leander photo, JM Gruber collection*

Super Dome cars were numbered 50 through 59 and had 68 seats in the upstairs dome. This view shows the lower level cafe-lounge. Booths were upholstered with green or gold top-grain leather and were arranged in two's, four's and five's to seat 28 people. *Author's collection*

Eastbound Morning Hiawatha with Skytop observation car leaving Portage, Wisconsin on a cold winter day, February 2, 1969. *JM Gruber collection*

Westbound Hiawatha No.101, Atlantic 4-4-2 at Portage, Wisconsin. *Ernest Mueller photo*

Eastbound Hiawatha No.100 with F7 Hudson leading, carrying flags for the following section, meets L3 Mikado 341 at Wisconsin Dells. *Ernest Mueller photo*

Eastbound Hiawatha No.100, Atlantic 4-4-2 at Wisconsin Dells. Industrial designer Otto Kuhler contributed to the bold orange, maroon and gray Hiawatha color scheme. *Ernest Mueller photo*

Scenic Wisconsin Dells was a stop on the Chicago-Twin Cities route. In July 1955, EMD FP7A-F7B-F7B, were leading the westbound Hiawatha across the Wisconsin River Bridge. *JM Gruber collection*

Westbound Hiawatha Super Dome and diner car crossing the Wisconsin River Bridge at Wisconsin Dells, July 1955. *JM Gruber collection*

Westbound Skytop observation car on the end of Chicago-Twin Cities Hiawatha at Wisconsin Dells, July 1955. *JM Gruber collection*

Milwaukee Road travel brochures for Wisconsin Dells and overnight train Pioneer Limited. *Author's collection*

91-A fronts westbound Hiawatha at Wisconsin Dells. Note the Dell View Hotel shuttle complete with greeter wearing Indian headdress, July 1955. *JM Gruber collection*

Milwaukee Road EMD FP7 100-A leads westbound Hiawatha at Mauston, Wisconsin in 1952. *JM Gruber collection*

The Skytop cars featured a convex rear with glass-framed panels extending from the window level to the roof. Skytop car "Priest Rapids" trailing the westbound Hiawatha at Mauston, Wisconsin in 1952. *JM Gruber collection*

La Crosse, Wisconsin was always a busy railroad town with the CB&Q and Milwaukee Road changing crews there. On May 26, 1936, Milwaukee Road Atlantic 4-4-2 was being serviced. *JM Gruber collection*

On June 4, 1961, Milwaukee Road westbound No. 55 meets eastbound Olympian Hiawatha No. 16 south of Red Wing, Minnesota. *Bruce R. Meyer photo*

Milwaukee Road EMD E7 leads westbound Hiawatha at Red Wing, Minnesota. Note the classic brick depot behind the engineman. The depot still stands today and is used by Red Wing Chamber of Commerce and Amtrak. *JM Gruber collection*

101-A leads the Afternoon Hiawatha past Hiawatha Mill & Elevator near the Twin Cities in 1953. *JM Gruber collection*

CHICAGO and NORTH WESTERN RAILWAY SYSTEM

Chicago & North Western 1954 dining car menu showing the 400 on James J. Hill Stone Arch Bridge in Minneapolis. *Author's collection*

Eastbound Twin Cities Zephyr leaving St. Paul, Minnesota for Chicago, April 30, 1945. The Mississippi River is to the left of the train and the Minnesota State Capitol is in the upper right corner. *BNSF Archives*

Classic Burlington shovelnose diesel, Budd-built 9902 at St. Paul Union Depot, July 1936. *Grant Oaks photo, JM Gruber collection*

Shortest line · Rock Island · Quickest time

Minneapolis & St. Paul

to Des Moines · to Kansas City · to St. Louis

Lv. Minneapolis..	4.00 p. m.	10.20 p. m.
Lv. St. Paul	4.35 p. m.	11.10 p. m.
Ar. Des Moines...	12.05 a. m.	7.50 a. m.

Lv. Minneapolis..	4.00 p. m.	10.20 p. m.
Lv. St. Paul	4.35 p. m.	11.10 p. m.
Ar. Kansas City ..	7.20 a. m.	3.25 p. m.

Lv. Minneapolis..	8.30 a. m.	7.00 p. m.
Lv. St. Paul	9.10 a. m.	7.40 p. m.
Ar. St. Louis	7.12 a. m.	3.15 p. m.

R. E. KING, City Passenger Agent
Cor. 4th and Robert Streets, Phone Cedar 8633

THE SAINT PAUL
UNION DEPOT COMPANY

		DEPART. DATE_____		FARES
CB&Q	Lv._____	AM / PM	CST / CDT	
C.G.W.	Lv._____	AM / PM	CST / CDT	
CMSTP&P	Lv._____	AM / PM	CST / CDT	
CRI&P	Lv._____	AM / PM	CST / CDT	
G.N.	Lv._____	AM / PM	CST / CDT	
SOO LINE	Lv._____	AM / PM	CST / CDT	
N.P.	Lv._____	AM / PM	CST / CDT	
SPACE_____				
CAR NO._____				WE THANK YOU FOR YOUR PATRONAGE

St. Paul Union Depot ticket folder and Rock Island Lines ink blotter advertising Minneapolis and St. Paul trains. *Author's collection*

The Rock Island Line extended to the northernmost point of Minneapolis with the Twin Star Rocket (Minneapolis-Houston) and Zephyr Rocket (St. Paul-St. Louis). On June 19, 1969, Rock Island's Plainsman train No.18 (Twin Cities-Kansas City) was switching cars at St. Paul Union Depot. *JM Gruber collection*

America's Great Dome Luxury Train!

EMPIRE BUILDER

FASTEST...FINEST BETWEEN CHICAGO & SEATTLE

EMPIRE BUILDER

Connections: Make convenient connections on the Empire Builder with trains to the east and south in Chicago; trains to or from California in Seattle or Portland; air or ship to Hawaii or Alaska from Seattle or Vancouver, B.C.

For more information or reservations ask your travel agent or call or write Great Northern representatives located in principal cities of the U.S. and Canada—or write:

Passenger Traffic Manager
Great Northern Railway
St. Paul, Minnesota 55101

GREAT NORTHERN

6024-A   LITHO IN U.S.A.

GREAT NORTHERN

Great Northern travel brochure advertising new "Big Sky Blue" paint scheme on the 1967 Empire Builder. *Author's collection*

Great Northern Empire Builder had just arrived from Seattle at St. Paul Union Depot in 1947. *BNSF Archives*

The *Vista-Dome* North Coast Limited opens a new panorama of scenic beauty to travelers in the Northern Pacific West

Northern Pacific postcard showing Vista-Dome North Coast Limited. *Author's collection*

Northern Pacific's new diesel passenger locomotive 6500 was departing St. Paul Union Depot with the North Coast Limited when the engineer gave a wave to the photographer. *BNSF Archives*

Eastbound Atlantic 4-4-2 near St. Paul's Chestnut Street with the 1935 Hiawatha. *Robert Graham photo, JM Gruber collection*

Streamlined Hudson 4-6-4, departing St. Paul with eastbound Hiawatha No.100, December 10, 1938. *Robert Graham photo, JM Gruber collection*

Chicago & North Western E6 5005 built in 1941, leading the 400 at St. Paul, Minnesota, July 4, 1949. *Bill Raia collection*

Chicago & North Western eastbound 400 leaves Minneapolis, crossing the James J. Hill Stone Arch Bridge on a chilly April 21, 1935. *Robert Graham photo, Jay Williams collection*

The 1935 eastbound Hiawatha No.100, crossing the Mississippi River on the Short Line Bridge between Minneapolis and St. Paul. The bridge was double-track and 1,164-feet long. *Robert Graham photo, JM Gruber collection*

Twin Cities Zephyr crossing the James J. Hill Stone Arch Bridge headed into Great Northern Station in Minneapolis, July 20, 1948. The Stone Arch Bridge was built in 1883. The bridge is 2,100-feet long, 76-feet high, and is highlighted by 15 semi-circular stone arches, each spanning a distance of 80 feet. Today the bridge is a bike trail. *BNSF Archives*

Twin Cites Zephyr with Vista-Domes departing Great
Northern Station in Minneapolis for Chicago, April
1959. *Bill Raia collection*

Chicago & North Western E7 5018B switching its train at Great Northern Station in Minneapolis. The U.S. Post Office is to the left of the station and the Mississippi River is on the right, July 1953. *JM Gruber collection*

Great Northern Station in Minneapolis was always busy. In July 1953, C&NW switch engine No.94 was making up the Twin Cities 400. *JM Gruber collection*

Great Northern Station in Minneapolis shows the Twin Cities 400 observation car. Note the classic Great Northern "Rocky" heralds on the depot elevator shafts, used to lower mail and baggage to track level, seen here in July 1953. *JM Gruber collection*

Chicago & North Western E8 5025A with its train, ready to depart Great Northern Station in Minneapolis, July 1953. *JM Gruber collection*

Skytop Lounge

In addition to the Super Dome cars, the Twin Cities HIAWATHAS and the Olympian HIAWATHA also carry the glass-enclosed Skytop Lounge pictured above. These delightful observation rooms are still a unique feature of Milwaukee Road Hiawathas. Open to parlor car and private-room car passengers.

THE MILWAUKEE ROAD

Effective September 27, 1959

Train Schedules

CHICAGO · MILWAUKEE
LA CROSSE · WINONA
ST. PAUL · MINNEAPOLIS

SUPER DOMES

ON THE *Hiawathas*

THE **MILWAUKEE** ROAD

68-Passenger Super Dome

THE MILWAUKEE ROAD
Route of the Super Dome Hiawathas and Western "Cities" Streamliners

Milwaukee Road 1959 train schedules for Chicago-Twin Cities Hiawathas. *Author's collection*

Skytop observaton "Cedar Rapids" departing Minneapolis on the eastbound Hiawatha. The Skytops became the Hiawatha trademark. The car's sleek exterior and interior décor gave the impression of machine age speed and service. *JM Gruber collection*

Minneapolis' classic Milwaukee Road Station with train shed was built in 1898. It served Milwaukee Road, Soo Line and Rock Island trains. The station is located at 3rd and Washington Avenues in downtown Minneapolis and has been converted to a railroad theme Marriott Hotel. *Author's photo*

Milwaukee Road EMD E7 19 was ready to depart Minneapolis Station with an eastbound Hiawatha in 1953. The most striking feature of the station was the block-long train shed parallel to Washington Avenue. *JM Gruber collection*

Milwaukee Road's Minneapolis Station is the scene as coaches are ready for boarding on eastbound Hiawatha in 1953. Four tracks ran into the stub-end station. *JM Gruber collection*

Eastbound Hiawatha No.100 in Minneapolis with Beaver Tail observation car "Earling." The Beaver Tail design minimized wind resistance behind the fast moving train. *JM Gruber collection*

Amtrak had been in operation one year when this photo of St. Paul Union Depot was taken in 1972. A single baggage car near the depot symbolized the end of an era for private passenger train service to the Twin Cities. *Doug Wornom photo*

MORE TITLES FROM ICONOGRAFIX

AMERICAN CULTURE

COCA-COLA: A HISTORY IN PHOTOGRAPHS 1930-1969	ISBN 1-882256-46-8
COCA-COLA: ITS VEHICLES IN PHOTOGRAPHS 1930-1969	ISBN 1-882256-47-6
PHILLIPS 66 1945-1954 PHOTO ARCHIVE	ISBN 1-882256-42-5

AUTOMOTIVE

AMX PHOTO ARCHIVE: FROM CONCEPT TO REALITY	ISBN 1-58388-062-3
AUBURN AUTOMOBILES 1900-1936 PHOTO ARCHIVE	ISBN 1-58388-093-3
CAMARO 1967-2000 PHOTO ARCHIVE	ISBN 1-58388-032-1
CHEVROLET STATION WAGONS 1946-1966 PHOTO ARCHIVE	ISBN 1-58388-069-0
CLASSIC AMERICAN LIMOUSINES 1955-2000 PHOTO ARCHIVE	ISBN 1-58388-041-0
CORVAIR by CHEVROLET EXP. & PROD. CARS 1957-1969, LUDVIGSEN LIBRARY SERIES	ISBN 1-58388-058-5
CORVETTE THE EXOTIC EXPERIMENTAL CARS, LUDVIGSEN LIBRARY SERIES	ISBN 1-58388-017-8
CORVETTE PROTOTYPES & SHOW CARS PHOTO ALBUM	ISBN 1-882256-77-8
EARLY FORD V-8s 1932-1942 PHOTO ALBUM	ISBN 1-882256-97-2
FERRARI-THE FACTORY MARANELLO'S SECRETS 1950-1975, LUDVIGSEN LIB SERIES	ISBN 1-58388-085-2
FORD POSTWAR FLATHEADS 1946-1953 PHOTO ARCHIVE	ISBN 1-58388-080-1
IMPERIAL 1955-1963 PHOTO ARCHIVE	ISBN 1-882256-22-0
IMPERIAL 1964-1968 PHOTO ARCHIVE	ISBN 1-882256-23-9
JAVELIN PHOTO ARCHIVE: FROM CONCEPT TO REALITY	ISBN 1-58388-071-2
LINCOLN MOTOR CARS 1920-1942 PHOTO ARCHIVE	ISBN 1-882256-57-3
LINCOLN MOTOR CARS 1946-1960 PHOTO ARCHIVE	ISBN 1-882256-58-1
NASH 1936-1957 PHOTO ARCHIVE	ISBN 1-58388-086-0
PACKARD MOTOR CARS 1935-1942 PHOTO ARCHIVE	ISBN 1-882256-44-1
PACKARD MOTOR CARS 1946-1958 PHOTO ARCHIVE	ISBN 1-882256-45-X
PONTIAC DREAM CARS, SHOW CARS & PROTOTYPES 1928-1998 PHOTO ALBUM	ISBN 1-882256-93-X
PONTIAC FIREBIRD TRANS-AM 1969-1999 PHOTO ALBUM	ISBN 1-882256-95-6
PONTIAC FIREBIRD 1967-2000 PHOTO HISTORY	ISBN 1-58388-028-3
RAMBLER 1950-1969 PHOTO ARCHIVE	ISBN 1-58388-078-X
STRETCH LIMOUSINES 1928-2001 PHOTO ARCHIVE	ISBN 1-58388-070-4
STUDEBAKER 1933-1942 PHOTO ARCHIVE	ISBN 1-882256-24-7
STUDEBAKER HAWK 1956-1964 PHOTO ARCHIVE	ISBN 1-58388-094-1
ULTIMATE CORVETTE TRIVIA CHALLENGE	ISBN 1-58388-035-6

BUSES

BUSES OF MOTOR COACH INDUSTRIES 1932-2000 PHOTO ARCHIVE	ISBN 1-58388-039-9
FAGEOL & TWIN COACH BUSES 1922-1956 PHOTO ARCHIVE	ISBN 1-58388-075-5
FLXIBLE TRANSIT BUSES 1953-1995 PHOTO ARCHIVE	ISBN 1-58388-053-4
GREYHOUND BUSES 1914-2000 PHOTO ARCHIVE	ISBN 1-58388-027-5
*MACK® BUSES 1900-1960 PHOTO ARCHIVE**	ISBN 1-58388-020-8
PREVOST BUSES 1924-2002 PHOTO ARCHIVE	ISBN 1-58388-083-6
TRAILWAYS BUSES 1936-2001 PHOTO ARCHIVE	ISBN 1-58388-029-1
TROLLEY BUSES 1913-2001 PHOTO ARCHIVE	ISBN 1-58388-057-7
YELLOW COACH BUSES 1923-1943 PHOTO ARCHIVE	ISBN 1-58388-054-2

EMERGENCY VEHICLES

AMERICAN AMBULANCE 1900-2002: AN ILLUSTRATED HISTORY	ISBN 1-58388-081-X
AMERICAN LAFRANCE 700 SERIES 1945-1952 PHOTO ARCHIVE	ISBN 1-882256-90-5
AMERICAN LAFRANCE 700 SERIES 1945-1952 PHOTO ARCHIVE VOLUME 2	ISBN 1-58388-025-9
AMERICAN LAFRANCE 700 & 800 SERIES 1953-1958 PHOTO ARCHIVE	ISBN 1-882256-91-3
AMERICAN LAFRANCE 900 SERIES 1958-1964 PHOTO ARCHIVE	ISBN 1-58388-002-X
CLASSIC SEAGRAVE 1935-1951 PHOTO ARCHIVE	ISBN 1-58388-034-8
CROWN FIRECOACH 1951-1985 PHOTO ARCHIVE	ISBN 1-58388-047-X
FIRE CHIEF CARS 1900-1997 PHOTO ALBUM	ISBN 1-882256-87-5
HAHN FIRE APPARATUS 1923-1990 PHOTO ARCHIVE	ISBN 1-58388-077-1
HEAVY RESCUE TRUCKS 1931-2000 PHOTO GALLERY	ISBN 1-58388-045-3
IMPERIAL FIRE APPARATUS 1969-1976 PHOTO ARCHIVE	ISBN 1-58388-091-7
INDUSTRIAL AND PRIVATE FIRE APPARATUS 1925-2001 PHOTO ARCHIVE	ISBN 1-58388-049-6
LOS ANGELES CITY FIRE APPARATUS 1953-1999 PHOTO ARCHIVE	ISBN 1-58388-012-7
*MACK MODEL C FIRE TRUCKS 1957-1967 PHOTO ARCHIVE**	ISBN 1-58388-014-3
*MACK MODEL L FIRE TRUCKS 1940-1954 PHOTO ARCHIVE**	ISBN 1-882256-86-7
MAXIM FIRE APPARATUS 1914-1989 PHOTO ARCHIVE	ISBN 1-58388-050-X
NAVY & MARINE CORPS FIRE APPARATUS 1836 -2000 PHOTO GALLERY	ISBN 1-58388-031-3
PIERRE THIBAULT LTD. FIRE APPARATUS 1918-1990 PHOTO ARCHIVE	ISBN 1-58388-074-7
PIRSCH FIRE APPARATUS 1890-1991 PHOTO ARCHIVE	ISBN 1-58388-082-8
POLICE CARS: RESTORING, COLLECTING & SHOWING AMERICA'S FINEST SEDANS	ISBN 1-58388-046-1
SEAGRAVE 70TH ANNIVERSARY SERIES PHOTO ARCHIVE	ISBN 1-58388-001-1
TASC FIRE APPARATUS 1946-1985 PHOTO ARCHIVE	ISBN 1-58388-065-8
VOLUNTEER & RURAL FIRE APPARATUS PHOTO GALLERY	ISBN 1-58388-005-4
W.S. DARLEY & CO. FIRE APPARATUS 1908-2000 PHOTO ARCHIVE	ISBN 1-58388-061-5
WARD LAFRANCE FIRE TRUCKS 1918-1978 PHOTO ARCHIVE	ISBN 1-58388-013-5
WILDLAND FIRE APPARATUS 1940-2001 PHOTO GALLERY	ISBN 1-58388-056-9
YOUNG FIRE EQUIPMENT 1932-1991 PHOTO ARCHIVE	ISBN 1-58388-015-1

RACING

CHAPARRAL CAN-AM RACING CARS FROM TEXAS LUDVIGSEN LIBRARY SERIES	ISBN 1-58388-066-6
DRAG RACING FUNNY CARS OF THE 1970s PHOTO ARCHIVE	ISBN 1-58388-068-2
EL MIRAGE IMPRESSIONS: DRY LAKES LAND SPEED RACING	ISBN 1-58388-059-3
GT40 PHOTO ARCHIVE	ISBN 1-882256-64-6
INDY CARS OF THE 1950s, LUDVIGSEN LIBRARY SERIES	ISBN 1-58388-018-6
INDY CARS OF THE 1960s, LUDVIGSEN LIBRARY SERIES	ISBN 1-58388-052-6
INDIANAPOLIS RACING CARS OF FRANK KURTIS 1941-1963 PHOTO ARCHIVE	ISBN 1-58388-026-7
JUAN MANUEL FANGIO WORLD CHAMPION DRIVER SERIES PHOTO ALBUM	ISBN 1-58388-008-9
LOST RACE TRACKS TREASURES OF AUTOMOBILE RACING	ISBN 1-58388-084-4
MARIO ANDRETTI WORLD CHAMPION DRIVER SERIES PHOTO ALBUM	ISBN 1-58388-009-7
MERCEDES-BENZ 300SL RACING CARS 1952-1953 LUDVIGSEN LIBRARY SERIES	ISBN 1-58388-067-4
NOVI V-8 INDY CARS 1941-1965 LUDVIGSEN LIBRARY SERIES	ISBN 1-58388-037-2
PORSCHE SPYDERS TYPE 550 1953-1956, LUDVIGSEN LIBRARY SERIES	ISBN 1-58388-092-5
SEBRING 12-HOUR RACE 1970 PHOTO ARCHIVE	ISBN 1-882256-20-4
VANDERBILT CUP RACE 1936 & 1937 PHOTO ARCHIVE	ISBN 1-882256-66-2

RAILWAYS

CHICAGO, ST. PAUL, MINNEAPOLIS & OMAHA RAILWAY 1880-1940 PHOTO ARCHIVE	ISBN 1-882256-67-0
CHICAGO & NORTH WESTERN RAILWAY 1975-1995 PHOTO ARCHIVE	ISBN 1-882256-76-X
GREAT NORTHERN RAILWAY 1945-1970 VOL 2 PHOTO ARCHIVE	ISBN 1-882256-79-4
GREAT NORTHERN RAILWAY ORE DOCKS OF LAKE SUPERIOR PHOTO ARCHIVE	ISBN 1-58388-073-9
ILLINOIS CENTRAL RAILROAD 1854-1960 PHOTO ARCHIVE	ISBN 1-58388-063-1
MILWAUKEE ROAD 1850-1960 PHOTO ARCHIVE	ISBN 1-882256-61-1
MILWAUKEE ROAD DEPOTS 1856-1954 PHOTO ARCHIVE	ISBN 1-58388-040-2
SHOW TRAINS OF THE 20TH CENTURY	ISBN 1-58388-030-5
SOO LINE 1975-1992 PHOTO ARCHIVE	ISBN 1-882256-68-9
STREAMLINERS to the TWIN CITIES PHOTO ARCHIVE 400, Twin Zephyrs & Hiawatha Trains	ISBN 1-58388-096-8
TRAINS OF THE TWIN PORTS PHOTO ARCHIVE, DULUTH-SUPERIOR IN THE 1950s	ISBN 1-58388-003-8
TRAINS OF THE CIRCUS 1872-1956	ISBN 1-58388-024-0
TRAINS of the UPPER MIDWEST PHOTO ARCHIVE STEAM & DIESEL in the 1950s & 1960s	ISBN 1-58388-036-4
WISCONSIN CENTRAL LIMITED 1987-1996 PHOTO ARCHIVE	ISBN 1-882256-75-1
WISCONSIN CENTRAL RAILWAY 1871-1909 PHOTO ARCHIVE	ISBN 1-882256-78-6

TRUCKS

AUTOCAR TRUCKS 1950-1987 PHOTO ARCHIVE	ISBN 1-58388-072-0
BEVERAGE TRUCKS 1910-1975 PHOTO ARCHIVE	ISBN 1-882256-60-3
*BROCKWAY TRUCKS 1948-1961 PHOTO ARCHIVE**	ISBN 1-882256-55-7
CHEVROLET EL CAMINO PHOTO HISTORY INCL GMC SPRINT & CABALLERO	ISBN 1-58388-044-5
CIRCUS AND CARNIVAL TRUCKS 1923-2000 PHOTO ARCHIVE	ISBN 1-58388-048-8
DODGE B-SERIES TRUCKS RESTORER'S & COLLECTOR'S REFERENCE GUIDE & HISTORY	ISBN 1-58388-087-9
DODGE PICKUPS 1939-1978 PHOTO ALBUM	ISBN 1-882256-82-4
DODGE POWER WAGONS 1940-1980 PHOTO ARCHIVE	ISBN 1-882256-89-1
DODGE POWER WAGON PHOTO HISTORY	ISBN 1-58388-019-4
DODGE RAM TRUCKS 1994-2001 PHOTO HISTORY	ISBN 1-58388-051-8
DODGE TRUCKS 1929-1947 PHOTO ARCHIVE	ISBN 1-882256-36-0
DODGE TRUCKS 1948-1960 PHOTO ARCHIVE	ISBN 1-882256-37-9
FORD 4X4s 1935-1990 PHOTO HISTORY	ISBN 1-58388-079-8
FORD HEAVY-DUTY TRUCKS 1948-1998 PHOTO HISTORY	ISBN 1-58388-043-7
FREIGHTLINER TRUCKS 1937-1981 PHOTO ARCHIVE	ISBN 1-58388-090-9
JEEP 1941-2000 PHOTO ARCHIVE	ISBN 1-58388-021-6
JEEP PROTOTYPES & CONCEPT VEHICLES PHOTO ARCHIVE	ISBN 1-58388-033-X
*MACK MODEL AB PHOTO ARCHIVE**	ISBN 1-882256-18-2
*MACK AP SUPER-DUTY TRUCKS 1926-1938 PHOTO ARCHIVE**	ISBN 1-882256-54-9
*MACK MODEL B 1953-1966 VOL 2 PHOTO ARCHIVE**	ISBN 1-882256-34-4
*MACK EB-EC-ED-EE-EF-EG-DE 1936-1951 PHOTO ARCHIVE**	ISBN 1-882256-29-8
*MACK EH-EJ-EM-EQ-ER-ES 1936-1950 PHOTO ARCHIVE**	ISBN 1-882256-39-5
*MACK FC-FCSW-NW 1936-1947 PHOTO ARCHIVE**	ISBN 1-882256-28-X
*MACK FG-FH-FJ-FK-FN-FP-FT-FW 1937-1950 PHOTO ARCHIVE**	ISBN 1-882256-35-2
*MACK LF-LH-LJ-LM-LT 1940-1956 PHOTO ARCHIVE**	ISBN 1-882256-38-7
*MACK TRUCKS PHOTO GALLERY**	ISBN 1-882256-88-3
NEW CAR CARRIERS 1910-1998 PHOTO ALBUM	ISBN 1-882256-98-0
PLYMOUTH COMMERCIAL VEHICLES PHOTO ARCHIVE	ISBN 1-58388-004-6
REFUSE TRUCKS PHOTO ARCHIVE	ISBN 1-58388-042-9
RVs & CAMPERS 1900-2000: AN ILLUSTRATED HISTORY	ISBN 1-58388-064-X
STUDEBAKER TRUCKS 1927-1940 PHOTO ARCHIVE	ISBN 1-882256-40-9
WHITE TRUCKS 1900-1937 PHOTO ARCHIVE	ISBN 1-882256-80-8

TRACTORS & CONSTRUCTION EQUIPMENT

CASE TRACTORS 1912-1959 PHOTO ARCHIVE	ISBN 1-882256-32-8
CATERPILLAR PHOTO GALLERY	ISBN 1-882256-70-0
CATERPILLAR POCKET GUIDE THE TRACK-TYPE TRACTORS 1925-1957	ISBN 1-58388-022-4
CATERPILLAR D-2 & R-2 PHOTO ARCHIVE	ISBN 1-882256-99-9
CATERPILLAR D-8 1933-1974 PHOTO ARCHIVE INCLUDING DIESEL 75 & RD-8	ISBN 1-882256-96-4
CATERPILLAR MILITARY TRACTORS VOLUME 1 PHOTO ARCHIVE	ISBN 1-882256-16-6
CATERPILLAR MILITARY TRACTORS VOLUME 2 PHOTO ARCHIVE	ISBN 1-882256-17-4
CATERPILLAR SIXTY PHOTO ARCHIVE	ISBN 1-882256-05-0
CATERPILLAR TEN PHOTO ARCHIVE INCLUDING 7C FIFTEEN & HIGH FIFTEEN	ISBN 1-58388-011-9
CATERPILLAR THIRTY PHOTO ARCHIVE 2ND ED. INC. BEST THIRTY, 6G THIRTY & R-4	ISBN 1-58388-006-2
CIRCUS & CARNIVAL TRACTORS 1930-2001 PHOTO ARCHIVE	ISBN 1-58388-076-3
CLETRAC AND OLIVER CRAWLERS PHOTO ARCHIVE	ISBN 1-882256-43-3
CLASSIC AMERICAN STEAMROLLERS 1871-1935 PHOTO ARCHIVE	ISBN 1-58388-038-0
FARMALL CUB PHOTO ARCHIVE	ISBN 1-882256-71-9
FARMALL F-SERIES PHOTO ARCHIVE	ISBN 1-882256-02-6
FARMALL MODEL H PHOTO ARCHIVE	ISBN 1-882256-03-4
FARMALL MODEL M PHOTO ARCHIVE	ISBN 1-882256-15-8
FARMALL REGULAR PHOTO ARCHIVE	ISBN 1-882256-14-X
FARMALL SUPER SERIES PHOTO ARCHIVE	ISBN 1-882256-49-2
FORDSON 1917-1928 PHOTO ARCHIVE	ISBN 1-882256-33-6
HART-PARR PHOTO ARCHIVE	ISBN 1-882256-08-5
HOLT TRACTORS PHOTO ARCHIVE	ISBN 1-882256-10-7
INTERNATIONAL TRACTRACTOR PHOTO ARCHIVE	ISBN 1-882256-48-4
JOHN DEERE MODEL A PHOTO ARCHIVE	ISBN 1-882256-12-3
JOHN DEERE MODEL D PHOTO ARCHIVE	ISBN 1-882256-00-X
MARION CONSTRUCTION MACHINERY 1884-1975 PHOTO ARCHIVE	ISBN 1-58388-060-7
MARION MINING & DREDGING MACHINES PHOTO ARCHIVE	ISBN 1-58388-088-7
OLIVER TRACTORS PHOTO ARCHIVE	ISBN 1-882256-09-3
RUSSELL GRADERS PHOTO ARCHIVE	ISBN 1-882256-11-5
TWIN CITY TRACTOR PHOTO ARCHIVE	ISBN 1-882256-06-9

*THIS PRODUCT IS SOLD UNDER LICENSE FROM MACK TRUCKS, INC. MACK IS A REGISTERED TRADEMARK OF MACK TRUCKS, INC. ALL RIGHTS RESERVED.

All Iconografix books are available from direct mail specialty book dealers and bookstores worldwide, or can be ordered from the publisher. For book trade and distribution information or to add your name to our mailing list and receive a **FREE CATALOG** contact:

Iconografix, PO Box 446, Dept BK, Hudson, Wisconsin, 54016 Telephone: (715) 381-9755, (800) 289-3504 (USA), Fax: (715) 381-9756

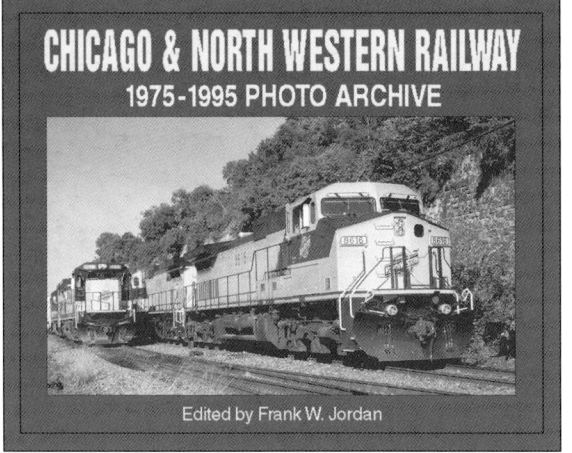